LET'S see

The White House

by Susan H. Gray

Content Adviser: Professor Sherry L. Field, Department of Social Science Education,

College of Education, The University of Georgia

Reading Adviser: Dr. Linda D. Labbo, Department of Reading Education,

College of Education, The University of Georgia

Compass Point Books

Minneapolis, Minnesota

Compass Point Books
3722 West 50th Street, #115
Minneapolis, MN 55410

Visit Compass Point Books on the Internet at *www.compasspointbooks.com* or e-mail your
request to *custserv@compasspointbooks.com*

Photographs ©: Photri-Microstock, cover, 4, 14, 16, 18; Stock Montage, 6, 12; The Maryland Historical, Baltimore,
Maryland, 8; North Wind Picture Archives, 10; Reuters/Win McNamee/Archive Photos, 20.

Editors: E. Russell Primm, Emily J. Dolbear, and Deborah Cannarella
Photo Researcher: Svetlana Zhurkina
Photo Selector: Linda S. Koutris
Designer: Melissa Voda

Library of Congress Cataloging-in-Publication Data
Gray, Susan Heinrichs.
    The White House / by Susan H. Gray.
      p. cm. — (Let's see library. Our nation)
    Includes bibliographical references (p.) and index.
    ISBN 0-7565-0145-8 (hardcover : library bind.)
    1. White House (Washington, D.C.)—Juvenile literature. 2. White House (Washington, D.C.)—History—
Juvenile literature. 3. Presidents—United States—Biography—Anecdotes—Juvenile literature. 4. Washington
(D.C.)—Buildings, structures, etc.—Juvenile literature. [1. White House (Washington, D.C.)] I. Title. II. Series.
    F204.W5 G73 2001
    975.3—dc21   2001001587

Table of Contents

What Is the White House?

How many rooms are in the house where you live? Imagine a house with more than 100 rooms! The **president** of the United States lives in a house that has 132 rooms. It is called the White House. The White House is on a wide street in a big city. The name of the street is Pennsylvania Avenue. The name of the city is Washington, D.C.

◄ *The White House in the spring*

Who Lives in the White House?

The president does not live all by himself in this big house. His family and pets live there too. More than forty presidents have lived in the White House. Many children have played in its rooms. One was Russell Harrison. He had a pet goat. One day, the goat ran away. His father, Benjamin Harrison, ran down Pennsylvania Avenue to catch it. Theodore Roosevelt had young children when he was president. His son, Quentin, kept a pony on the lawn.

◄ *Quentin Roosevelt on the lawn of the White House*

Who Built the White House?

George Washington was our first president, but he did not live in the White House. He lived in his own house. One day, some of his **advisers** came to him. They thought the president should live in a special home. However, they needed a **plan** to build the house. The president held a contest to see who came up with the best plan. Nine men entered the contest, including James Hoban. He had the best drawing. He won the contest. His prize was a gold medal.

◀ *The final plan for the White House was finished in 1793.*

How Long Did It Take to Build the White House?

President Washington picked the place to build the White House. He chose a spot near the Potomac River. The place looked awful. Pigs were asleep in the street. Weeds grew everywhere. So people got to work. They cleared the land for the White House. Some men got the boards. Some men made the bricks. It took eight years to build the White House. It was the biggest house in the country. By that time, the United States had a new president. John Adams was the first president to live in the White House.

◄ *The Potomac River before Washington, D.C., was built*

Who Planted the Trees and Gardens?

Thomas Jefferson was America's third president. He loved gardens. He built beautiful gardens around the White House. He also planted trees. He was the first president to invite the public to visit the White House. Today, people come from all around the world to see our president's home.

Many other presidents planted gardens too. President Woodrow Wilson had a vegetable garden. His family ate the food that grew there. He also raised sheep in the yard! He sold the sheep's wool. The money helped to build hospitals for soldiers during World War I.

◄ *Sheep grazed on the White House lawn during World War I.*

Who Set the White House on Fire?

In 1814, there was a terrible fire at the White House. The United States was at war with Great Britain. President James Madison lived in the White House with his wife, Dolley. The British army was marching to Washington, D.C. The president knew that it was not safe to stay. Dolley took a big picture of George Washington off the wall. Then she ran outside with it.

The British army set the White House on fire. Soon, it started to rain. The rain put out the fire, but the White House was a mess! It took three years to fix up the house.

◄ *The British army burned the White House in 1814.*

What Special Rooms Are in the White House?

The White House has 132 rooms, 32 bathrooms, and three elevators. Many of the rooms in the White House have special names. There is a Red Room and a Green Room. Each year, the Christmas tree is set up in the Blue Room.

The East Room is the biggest room in the house. Dances and parties are held there. A big picture of George Washington hangs on the wall. It is the picture that Dolley Madison saved from the fire.

Where Does the President Work?

The president works in the Oval Office. He signs papers and meets with visitors there. Each new president picks the desk he will use. Many presidents have used a desk made from the wood of an old British ship. Queen Victoria of Great Britain gave the desk to President Rutherford B. Hayes.

◄ *George Bush worked in the Oval Office at the desk given to the United States by Queen Victoria.*

What Does the White House Mean to Me?

The White House is an important place. It is the most famous house in the United States and the home of the president.

The White House has many special events for visitors. One event is the Easter Egg Roll. It happens every year on the morning after Easter. Boys and girls come to the White House very early. Each child gets one Easter egg. The children roll their eggs on the White House lawn. Even the president watches the race!

Every day, many people visit the White House. Maybe, one day, you will visit this famous house.

◄ *Boys and girls roll Easter eggs on the White House lawn.*

Glossary

advisers—people who help others make decisions

plan—a drawing of something before it is built

president—the elected leader of a country

Did You Know?

• About 6,000 people visit the White House each day.

• It takes 570 gallons (2,158 liters) of paint to paint the White House.

• John Kennedy Jr. was the son of our thirty-fifth president. He used to play under his father's desk in the Oval Office. The desk had a secret door.

• When the first astronauts landed on the moon, Richard Nixon was president. He talked to the astronauts from the Oval Office.

Want to Know More?

At the Library

Binns, Tristan Boyer. *The White House*. Chicago: Heinemann Library, 2001.

Griest, Lisa. *Lost at the White House: A 1909 Easter Story*. Minneapolis: Carolrhoda, 1994.

Waters, Kate. *The Story of the White House*. New York: Scholastic, 1992.

On the Web

The White House

http://www.whitehouse.gov/kids

For an online tour of the White House and many fun activities

The White House Historical Association

http://www.whitehousehistory.org

For photos and facts about each of the forty-three presidents of the United States

Through the Mail

White House Historical Association

740 Jackson Place, N.W.

Washington, DC 20503

202/737-8292

For information about special programs, films, and the art in the White House collection

On the Road

The White House

1600 Pennsylvania Avenue, N.W.

Washington, DC 20500

202/456-7041

For information about tours and more, call 202/456-7041. The White House is closed to tours on Sunday and Monday.

Index

About the Author
Susan H. Gray holds bachelor's and master's degrees in zoology from the University of Arkansas in Fayetteville. She has taught classes in general biology, human anatomy, and physiology. She has also worked as a freshwater biologist and scientific illustrator. In her twenty years as a writer, Susan H. Gray has covered many topics and written a variety of science books for children.